Heaven and Hell

Heaven and Hell

by
ALDOUS HUXLEY

PERENNIAL LIBRARY
Harper & Row, Publishers
New York, Evanston, San Francisco, London

In the history of science the collector of specimens preceded the zoologist and followed the exponents of natural theology and magic. He had ceased to study animals in the spirit of the authors of the bestiaries, for whom the ant was incarnate industry, the panther an emblem, surprisingly enough, of Christ, the polecat a shocking example of uninhibited lasciviousness. But, except in a rudimentary way, he was not yet a physiologist, ecologist or student of animal behavior. His primary concern was to make a census, to catch, kill, stuff and describe as many kinds of beasts as he could lay his hands on.

Like the earth of a hundred years ago, our mind still has its darkest Africas, its unmapped Borneos and Amazonian basins. In relation to the fauna of these regions we are not yet zoologists, we are mere naturalists and collectors of specimens. The fact is unfortunate; but we have to accept it, we have to make the best of it. However lowly, the work of the collector must be done, before we can proceed to the higher scientific tasks of classification, analysis, experiment and theory making.

Like the giraffe and the duckbilled platypus, the creatures inhabiting these remoter regions of the mind are exceedingly improbable. Nevertheless they exist, they are facts of observation; and as such, they cannot be ignored by anyone who is honestly trying to understand the world in which he lives.

It is difficult, it is all but impossible, to speak of mental events except in similes drawn from the more familiar universe of material things. If I have made use of geographical and zoological metaphors, it is not wantonly, out of a mere addiction to picturesque language. It is because such metaphors express very forcibly the essential otherness of the mind's far continents, the complete autonomy and self-sufficiency of their inhabitants. A man consists of what I may call an Old World of personal consciousness and, beyond a dividing sea, a series of New Worlds—the not too distant Virginias and Carolinas of the personal subconscious and the vegetative soul; the Far West of the collective unconscious, with its flora of symbols, its tribes of aboriginal archetypes; and, across another, vaster ocean, at the antipodes of everyday consciousness, the world of Visionary Experience.

If you go to New South Wales, you will see marsupials hopping about the countryside. And if you go to the antipodes of the self-conscious mind, you will encounter all sorts of creatures at least as odd

as kangaroos. You do not invent these creatures any
more than you invent marsupials. They live their
own lives in complete independence. A man cannot
control them. All he can do is to go to the mental
equivalent of Australia and look around him.

Some people never consciously discover their
antipodes. Others make an occasional landing. Yet
others (but they are few) find it easy to go and
come as they please. For the naturalist of the mind,
the collector of psychological specimens, the primary need is some safe, easy and reliable method
of transporting himself and others from the Old
World to the New, from the continent of familiar
cows and horses to the continent of a wallaby and
the platypus.

Two such methods exist. Neither of them is perfect; but both are sufficiently reliable, sufficiently
easy and sufficiently safe to justify their employ-
ment by those who know what they are doing. In
the first case the soul is transported to its far-off
destination by the aid of a chemical—either mescalin or lysergic acid. In the second case, the ve-
hicle is psychological in nature, and the passage to
the mind's antipodes is accomplished by hypnosis.
The two vehicles carry the consciousness to the
same region; but the drug has the longer range and
takes its passengers further into the *terra incog-
nita.**

How and why does hypnosis produce its observed effects? We do not know. For our present

* See Appendix I, page 53.

purposes, however, we do not have to know. All
that is necessary, in this context, is to record the
fact that some hypnotic subjects are transported,
in the trance state, to a region in the mind's antipodes, where they find the equivalent of marsupials
—strange psychological creatures leading an autonomous existence according to the law of their
own being.

About the physiological effects of mescalin we
know a little. Probably (for we are not yet certain)
it interferes with the enzyme system that regulates
cerebral functioning. By doing so it lowers the efficiency of the brain as an instrument for focusing
the mind on the problems of life on the surface of
our planet. This lowering of what may be called the
biological efficiency of the brain seems to permit
the entry into consciousness of certain classes of
mental events, which are normally excluded, because they possess no survival value. Similar intru-
sions of biologically useless, but aesthetically and
sometimes spiritually valuable material may occur
as the result of illness or fatigue; or they may be induced by fasting, or a period of confinement in a
place of darkness and complete silence.°

A person under the influence of mescalin or lysergic acid will stop seeing visions when given a
large dose of nicotinic acid. This helps to explain
the effectiveness of fasting as an inducer of visionary experience. By reducing the amount of avail-
able sugar, fasting lowers the brain's biological

° See Appendix II, page 58.

efficiency and so makes possible the entry into consciousness of material possessing no survival value. Moreover, by causing a vitamin deficiency, it removes from the blood that known inhibitor of visions, nicotinic acid. Another inhibitor of visionary experience is ordinary, everyday, perceptual experience. Experimental psychologists have found that, if you confine a man to a "restricted environment," where there is no light, no sound, nothing to smell and, if you put him in a tepid bath, only one, almost imperceptible thing to touch, the victim will very soon start "seeing things," "hearing things" and having strange bodily sensations.

Milarepa, in his Himalayan cavern, and the anchorites of the Thebaid followed essentially the same procedure and got essentially the same results. A thousand pictures of the Temptations of St. Anthony bear witness to the effectiveness of restricted diet and restricted environment. Asceticism, it is evident, has a double motivation. If men and women torment their bodies, it is not only because they hope in this way to atone for past sins and avoid future punishments; it is also because they long to visit the mind's antipodes and do some visionary sightseeing. Empirically and from the reports of other ascetics, they know that fasting and a restricted environment will transport them where they long to go. Their self-inflicted punishment may be the door to paradise. (It may also—and this is a point which will be discussed in a later paragraph —be a door in the infernal regions.)

From the point of view of an inhabitant of the
Old World, marsupials are exceedingly odd. But
oddity is not the same as randomness. Kangaroos
and wallabies may lack verisimilitude; but their
improbability repeats itself and obeys recognizable
laws. The same is true of the psychological creatures inhabiting the remoter regions of our minds.
The experiences encountered under the influence of
mescalin or deep hypnosis are very strange; but
they are strange with a certain regularity, strange
according to a pattern.

What are the common features which this pattern
imposes upon our visionary experiences? First and
most important is the experience of light. Everything seen by those who visit the mind's antipodes
is brilliantly illuminated and seems to shine from
within. All colors are intensified to a pitch far beyond anything seen in the normal state, and at the
same time the mind's capacity for recognizing fine
distinctions of tone and hue is notably heightened.

In this respect there is a marked difference between these visionary experiences and ordinary
dreams. Most dreams are without color, or else are
only partially or feebly colored. On the other hand,
the visions met with under the influence of mescalin
or hypnosis are always intensely and, one might say,
preternaturally brilliant in color. Professor Calvin
Hall, who has collected records of many thousands
of dreams, tells us that about two-thirds of all
dreams are in black and white. "Only one dream in
three is colored, or has some color in it." A few peo-

ple dream entirely in color; a few never experience color in their dreams; the majority sometimes dream in color, but more often do not.

"We have come to the conclusion," writes Dr. Hall, "that color in dreams yields no information about the personality of the dreamer." I agree with this conclusion. Color in dreams and visions tells us no more about the personality of the beholder than does color in the external world. A garden in July is perceived as brightly colored. The perception tells us something about sunshine, flowers and butterflies, but little or nothing about our own selves. In the same way the fact that we see brilliant colors in our visions and in some of our dreams tells us something about the fauna of the mind's antipodes, but nothing whatever about the personality who inhabits what I have called the Old World of the mind.

Most dreams are concerned with the dreamer's private wishes and instinctive urges, and with the conflicts which arise when these wishes and urges are thwarted by a disapproving conscience or a fear of public opinion. The story of these drives and conflicts is told in terms of dramatic symbols, and in most dreams the symbols are uncolored. Why should this be the case? The answer, I presume, is that, to be effective, symbols do not require to be colored. The letters in which we write about roses need not be red, and we can describe the rainbow by means of ink marks on white paper. Textbooks are illustrated by line engravings and half-tone

plates; and these uncolored images and diagrams
effectively convey information.

What is good enough for the waking consciousness is evidently good enough for the personal subconscious, which finds it possible to express its
meanings through uncolored symbols. Color turns
out to be a kind of touchstone of reality. That
which is given is colored; that which our symbol-
creating intellect and fancy put together is uncolored. Thus the external world is perceived as colored. Dreams, which are not given but fabricated
by the personal subconscious, are generally in black
and white. (It is worth remarking that, in most
people's experience, the most brightly colored
dreams are those of landscapes, in which there is
no drama, no symbolic reference to conflict, merely
the presentation to consciousness of a given, non-
human fact.)

The images of the archetypal world are symbolic;
but since we, as individuals, do not fabricate them,
but find them "out there" in the collective uncon-
sciousness, they exhibit some at least of the charac-
teristics of given reality and are colored. The non-
symbolic inhabitants of the mind's antipodes exist
in their own right, and like the given facts of the
external world are colored. Indeed, they are far
more intensely colored than external data. This may
be explained, at least in part, by the fact that our
perceptions of the external world are habitually
clouded by the verbal notions in terms of which we
do our thinking. We are forever attempting to con-

vert things into signs for the more intelligible abstractions of our own invention. But in doing so, we rob these things of a great deal of their native thinghood.

At the antipodes of the mind, we are more or less completely free of language, outside the system of conceptual thought. Consequently our perception of visionary objects possesses all the freshness, all the naked intensity, of experiences which have never been verbalized, never assimilated to lifeless abstractions. Their color (that hallmark of givenness) shines forth with a brilliance which seems to us preternatural, because it is in fact entirely natural—entirely natural in the sense of being entirely unsophisticated by language or the scientific, philosophical and utilitarian notions, by means of which we ordinarily re-create the given world in our own drearily human image.

In his *Candle of Vision*, the Irish poet, Æ (George Russell), has analyzed his visionary experiences with remarkable acuity. "When I meditate," he writes, "I feel in the thoughts and images that throng about me the reflections of personality; but there are also windows in the soul, through which can be seen images created not by human but by the divine imagination."

Our linguistic habits lead us into error. For example, we are apt to say, "I imagine," when what we should have said is, "The curtain was lifted that I might see." Spontaneous or induced, visions are never our personal property. Memories belonging to the ordinary self have no place in them. The things seen are wholly unfamiliar. "There is no reference or resemblance," in Sir William Herschel's phrase, "to any objects recently seen or even thought of." When faces appear, they are never the faces of friends or acquaintances. We are out of the Old World, and exploring the antipodes.

For most of us most of the time, the world of everyday experience seems rather dim and drab. But for a few people often, and for a fair number occasionally, some of the brightness of visionary experience spills over, as it were, into common seeing, and the everyday universe is transfigured. Though still recognizably itself, the Old World takes on the quality of the mind's antipodes. Here is an entirely characteristic description of this transfiguration of the everyday world:

"I was sitting on the seashore, half listening to a friend arguing violently about something which merely bored me. Unconsciously to myself, I looked at a film of sand I had picked up on my hand, when I suddenly saw the exquisite beauty of every little grain of it; instead of being dull, I saw that each particle was made up on a perfect geometrical pattern, with sharp angles, from each of which a brilliant shaft of light was reflected, while each tiny crystal shone like a rainbow. . . . The rays crossed and recrossed, making exquisite patterns of such beauty that they left me breathless. . . . Then, suddenly, my consciousness was lighted up from within and I saw in a vivid way how the whole universe was made up of particles of material which, no matter how dull and lifeless they might seem, were nevertheless filled with this intense and vital beauty. For a second or two the whole world appeared as a blaze of glory. When it died down, it left me with something I have never forgotten and which constantly reminds me of the beauty locked up in every minute speck of material around us."

Similarly George Russell writes of seeing the world illumined by "an intolerable lustre of light"; of finding himself looking at "landscapes as lovely as a lost Eden"; of beholding a world where the "colors were brighter and purer, and yet made a softer harmony." Again, "the winds were sparkling and diamond clear, and yet full of color as an opal, as they glittered through the valley, and I knew the Golden Age was all about me, and it was we who had been blind to it, but that it had never passed away from the world."

Many similar descriptions are to be found in the poets and in the literature of religious mysticism. One thinks, for example, of Wordsworth's *Ode on the Intimations of Immortality in Childhood;* of certain lyrics by George Herbert and Henry Vaughan; of Traherne's *Centuries of Meditation;* of the passage in his autobiography, where Father Surin describes the miraculous transformation of an enclosed convent garden into a fragment of heaven.

Preternatural light and color are common to all visionary experiences. And along with light and color there goes, in every case, a recognition of heightened significance. The self-luminous objects which we see in the mind's antipodes possess a meaning, and this meaning is, in some sort, as intense as their color. Significance here is identical with being; for, at the mind's antipodes, objects do not stand for anything but themselves. The images which appear in the nearer reaches of the collective subconscious have meaning in relation to the basic facts of human experience; but here, at the limits of the visionary world, we are confronted by facts which, like the facts of external nature, are independent of man, both individually and collectively, and exist in their own right. And their meaning consists precisely in this, that they are intensely themselves and, being intensely themselves, are manifestations of the essential givenness, the non-human otherness of the universe.

Light, color and significance do not exist in isolation. They modify, or are manifested by, objects. Are there any special classes of objects common to most visionary experiences? The answer is: yes, there are. Under mescalin and hypnosis, as well as in spontaneous visions, certain classes of perceptual experiences turn up again and again.

The typical mescalin or lysergic-acid experience begins with perceptions of colored, moving, living geometrical forms. In time, pure geometry becomes concrete, and the visionary perceives, not patterns, but patterned things, such as carpets, carvings, mosaics. These give place to vast and complicated buildings, in the midst of landscapes, which change continuously, passing from richness to more intensely colored richness, from grandeur to deepening grandeur. Heroic figures, of the kind that Blake called "The Seraphim," may make their appearance, alone or in multitudes. Fabulous animals move across the scene. Everything is novel and amazing. Almost never does the visionary see anything that reminds him of his own past. He is not remembering scenes, persons or objects, and he is not inventing them; he is looking on at a new creation.

The raw material for this creation is provided by the visual experiences of ordinary life; but the molding of this material into forms is the work of someone who is most certainly not the self, who originally had the experiences, or who later recalled and reflected upon them. They are (to quote the words used by Dr. J. R. Smythies in a recent paper in the *American Journal of Psychiatry*) "the work of a highly differentiated mental compartment, without any apparent connection, emotional or volitional, with the aims, interests, or feelings of the person concerned."

Here, in quotation or condensed paraphrase, is Weir Mitchell's account of the visionary world to which he was transported by peyote, the cactus which is the natural souce of mescalin.

At his entry into that world he saw a host of "star points" and what looked like "fragments of stained glass." Then came "delicate floating films of color." These were displaced by an "abrupt rush of countless points of white light," sweeping across the field

of vision. Next there were zigzag lines of very bright
colors, which somehow turned into swelling clouds
of still more brilliant hues. Buildings now made
their appearance, and then landscapes. There was
a Gothic tower of elaborate design with worn
statues in the doorways or on stone brackets. "As I
gazed, every projecting angle, cornice and even
the faces of the stones at their joinings were by
degrees covered or hung with clusters of what
seemed to be huge precious stones, but uncut
stones, some being more like masses of transparent
fruit. . . . All seemed to possess an interior light."
The Gothic tower gave place to a mountain, a cliff
of inconceivable height, a colossal bird claw
carved in stone and projecting over the abyss, an
endless unfurling of colored draperies, and an ef-
florescence of more precious stones. Finally there
was a view of green and purple waves breaking on
a beach "with myriads of lights of the same tint as
the waves."

Every mescalin experience, every vision arising
under hypnosis, is unique; but all recognizably be-
long to the same species. The landscapes, the archi-
tectures, the clustering gems, the brilliant and intri-
cate patterns—these, in their atmosphere of preternatural light, preternatural color and preternatural significance, are the stuff of which the
mind's antipodes are made. Why this should be so,
we have no idea. It is a brute fact of experience
which, whether we like it or not, we have to accept
—just as we have to accept the fact of kangaroos.

From these facts of visionary experience let us
now pass to the accounts preserved in all the cul-
tural traditions, of Other Worlds—the worlds inhabited by the gods, by the spirits of the dead, by
man in his primal state of innocence.

Reading these accounts, we are immediately
struck by the close similarity between induced or
spontaneous visionary experiences and the heavens
and fairylands of folklore and religion. Preternatural light, preternatural intensity of coloring, preternatural significance—these are characteristic of
all the Other Worlds and Golden Ages. And in virtually every case this preternaturally significant
light shines on, or shines out of, a landscape of such
surpassing beauty that words cannot express it.

Thus in the Greco-Roman tradition we find the
lovely Garden of the Hesperides, the Elysian Plain,
and the fair Island of Leuke, to which Achilles was
translated. Memnon went to another luminous island, somewhere in the East. Odysseus and Pen-
elope traveled in the opposite direction and en-
joyed their immortality with Circe in Italy. Still
further to the west were the Islands of the Blest,
first mentioned by Hesiod and so firmly believed
in that, as late as the first century B.C., Sertorius
planned to send a squadron from Spain to discover
them.

Magically lovely islands reappear in the folklore
of the Celts and, at the opposite side of the world,
in that of the Japanese. And between Avalon in the
extreme West and Horaisan in the Far East, there

is the land of Uttarakuru, the Other World of the Hindus. "The land," we read in the *Ramayana*, "is watered by lakes with golden lotuses. There are rivers by thousands, full of leaves of the color of sapphire and lapis lazuli; and the lakes, resplendent like the morning sun, are adorned by golden beds of red lotus. The country all around is covered by jewels and precious stones, with gay beds of blue lotus, golden-petalled. Instead of sand, pearls, gems and gold form the banks of the rivers, which are overhung with trees of firebright gold. These trees perpetually bear flowers and fruit, give forth a sweet fragrance and abound with birds."

Uttarakuru, we see, resembles the landscapes of the mescalin experience in being rich with precious stones. And this characteristic is common to virtually all the Other Worlds of religious tradition. Every paradise abounds in gems, or at least in gemlike objects resembling, as Weir Mitchell puts it, "transparent fruit." Here, for example, is Ezekiel's version of the Garden of Eden. "Thou hast been in Eden, the garden of God. Every precious stone was thy covering, the sardius, topaz and the diamond, the beryl, the onyx and the jasper, the sapphire, the emerald and the carbuncle, and gold. . . . Thou art the anointed cherub that covereth . . . thou hast walked up and down in the midst of the stones of fire." The Buddhist paradises are adorned with similar "stones of fire." Thus, the Western Paradise of the Pure Land Sect is walled with silver, gold

and beryl; has lakes with jeweled banks and a profusion of glowing lotuses, within which the bodhisattvas sit enthroned.

In describing their Other Worlds, the Celts and
Teutons speak very little of precious stones, but
have much to say of another and, for them, equally
wonderful substance—glass. The Welsh had a
blessed land called Ynisvitrin, the Isle of Glass; and
one of the names of the Germanic kingdom of the
dead was Glasberg. One is reminded of the Sea of
Glass in the Apocalypse.

Most paradises are adorned with buildings, and,
like the trees, the waters, the hills and fields, these
buildings are bright with gems. We are familiar
with the New Jerusalem. "And the building of the
wall of it was of jasper, and the city was of pure
gold, like unto clear glass. . . . And the founda-
tions of the wall of the city were garnished with all
manner of precious stones."

Similar descriptions are to be found in the eschatological literature of Hinduism, Buddhism and
Islam. Heaven is always a place of gems. Why
should this be the case? Those who think of all human activities in terms of a social and economic
frame of reference will give some such answer as
this: Gems are very rare on earth. Few people possess them. To compensate themselves for these
facts, the spokesmen for the poverty-stricken majority have filled their imaginary heavens with
precious stones. This "pie in the sky" hypothesis

contains, no doubt, some element of truth; but it fails to explain why precious stones should have come to be regarded as precious in the first place.

Men have spent enormous amounts of time, energy and money on the finding, mining and cutting of colored pebbles. Why? The utilitarian can offer no explanation for such fantastic behavior. But as soon as we take into account the facts of visionary experience, everything becomes clear. In vision, men perceive a profusion of what Ezekiel calls "stones of fire," of what Weir Mitchell describes as "transparent fruit." These things are self-luminous, exhibit a preternatural brilliance of color and possess a preternatural significance. The material objects which most nearly resemble these sources of visionary illumination are gem stones. To acquire such a stone is to acquire something whose preciousness is guaranteed by the fact that it exists in the Other World.

Hence man's otherwise inexplicable passion for gems and hence his attribution to precious stones of therapeutic and magical virtue. The causal chain, I am convinced, begins in the psychological Other World of visionary experience, descends to earth and mounts again to the theological Other World of heaven. In this context the words of Socrates, in the *Phaedo*, take on a new significance. There exists, he tells us, an ideal world above and beyond the world of matter. "In this other earth the colors are much purer and much more brilliant than they are down here. . . . The very mountains, the very stones have a richer gloss, a lovelier transparency and intensity of hue. The precious stones of this lower world, our highly prized cornelians, jaspers, emeralds and all the rest, are but the tiny fragments of these stones above. In the other earth there is no stone but is precious and exceeds in beauty every gem of ours."

In other words, precious stones are precious because they bear a faint resemblance to the glowing marvels seen with the inner eye of the visionary. "The view of that world," says Plato, "is a vision of blessed beholders"; for to see things "as they are in themselves" is bliss unalloyed and inexpressible.

Among people who have no knowledge of precious stones or of glass, heaven is adorned not with minerals, but flowers. Preternaturally brilliant flowers bloom in most of the Other Worlds described by primitive eschatologists, and even in the begemmed and glassy paradises of the more advanced religions they have their place. One remembers the lotus of Hindu and Buddhist tradition, the roses and lilies of the West.

"God first planted a garden." The statement expresses a deep psychological truth. Horticulture has its source—or at any rate one of its sources—in the Other World of the mind's antipodes. When worshipers offer flowers at the altar, they are returning to the gods things which they know, or (if they are not visionaries) obscurely feel, to be indigenous to heaven.

And this return to the source is not merely symbolical; it is also a matter of immediate experience. For the traffic between our Old World and its antipodes, between Here and Beyond, travels along a two-way street. Gems, for example, come from the soul's visionary heaven; but they also lead the soul back to that heaven. Contemplating them, men find themselves (as the phrase goes) *transported*—carried away toward that Other Earth of the Platonic dialogue, that magical place where every pebble is a precious stone. And the same effects may be produced by artifacts of glass and metal, by tapers burning in the dark, by brilliantly colored images and ornaments; by flowers, shells and feathers; by landscapes seen, as Shelly from the Euganean Hills saw Venice, in the transfiguring light of dawn or sunset.

Indeed, we may risk a generalization and say that whatever, in nature or in a work of art, resembles one of those intensely significant, inwardly glowing objects encountered at the mind's antipodes is capable of inducing, if only in a partial and attenuated form, the visionary experience. At this point a hypnotist will remind us that, if he can be induced to stare intently at a shiny object, a patient may go into trance; and that if he goes into trance, or if he goes only into reverie, he may very well see visions within and a transfigured world without.

But how, precisely, and why does the view of a shiny object induce a trance or a state of reverie? Is it, as the Victorians maintained, a simple matter of eye strain resulting in general nervous exhaustion? Or shall we explain the phenomenon in purely psychological terms—as concentration pushed to the point of mono-ideism and leading to dissociation?

And there is a third possibility. Shiny objects may remind our unconscious of what it enjoys at the mind's antipodes, and these obscure intimations of life in the Other World are so fascinating that we pay less attention to this world and so become capable of experiencing consciously something of that which, unconsciously, is always with us.

We see then that there are in nature certain scenes, certain classes of objects, certain materials, possessed of the power to transport the beholder's mind in the direction of its antipodes, out of the everyday Here and toward the Other World of Vision. Similarly, in the realm of art, we find certain works, even certain classes of works, in which the same transporting power is manifest. These vision-inducing works may be executed in vision-inducing materials, such as glass, metal, gems, or gem-like pigments. In other cases their power is due to the fact that they render, in some peculiarly expressive way, some transporting scene or object.

The best vision-inducing art is produced by men and women who have themselves had the visionary experience; but it is also possible for any reasonably good artist, simply by following an approved recipe, to create works which shall have at least some transporting power.

Of all the vision-inducing arts that which depends

most completely on its raw materials is, of course,
the art of the goldsmith and jeweler. Polished
metals and precious stones are so intrinsically
transporting that even a Victorian, even an *art nouveau* jewel is a thing of power. And when to this
natural magic of glinting metal and self-luminous
stone is added the other magic of noble forms and
colors artfully blended, we find ourselves in the
presence of a genuine talisman.

Religious art has always and everywhere made
use of these vision-inducing materials. The shrine
of gold, the chryselephantine statue, the jeweled
symbol or image, the glittering furniture of the
altar—we find these things in contemporary Europe as in ancient Egypt, in India and China as
among the Greeks, the Incas, the Aztecs.

The products of the goldsmith's art are intrinsically numinous. They have their place at the very
heart of every Mystery, in every holy of holies. This
sacred jewelry has always been associated with the
light of lamps and candles. For Ezekiel, a gem was
a stone of fire. Conversely, a flame is a living gem,
endowed with all the transporting power that be-
longs to the precious stone and, to a lesser degree,
to polished metal. This transporting power of flame
increases in proportion to the depth and extent of
the surrounding darkness. The most impressively
numinous temples are caverns of twilight, in which
a few tapers give life to the transporting, other-
worldly treasures on the altar.

Glass is hardly less effective as an inducer of

visions than are the natural gems. In certain re-
spects, indeed, it is more effective, for the simple
reason that there is more of it. Thanks to glass, a
whole building—the Sainte Chapelle, for example,
the cathedrals of Chartres and Sens—could be
turned into something magical and transporting.
Thanks to glass, Paolo Uccello could design a circu-
lar jewel thirteen feet in diameter—his great win-
dow of the Resurrection, perhaps the most extraordinary single work of vision-inducing art ever produced.

For the men of the Middle Ages, it is evident,
visionary experience was supremely valuable. So
valuable, indeed, that they were ready to pay for it
in hard-earned cash. In the twelfth century col-
lecting boxes were placed in the churches for the
upkeep and installation of stained-glass windows.
Suger, the Abbot of St. Denis, tells us that they
were always full.

But self-respecting artists cannot be expected to
go on doing what their fathers have already done
supremely well. In the fourteenth century color
gave place to grisaille, and windows ceased to be
vision inducing. When, in the later fifteenth century, color came into fashion again, the glass painters felt the desire, and found themselves, at the
same time, technically equipped, to imitate Renaissance painting in transparency. The results were
often interesting; but they were not transporting.

Then came the Reformation. The Protestants dis-
approved of visionary experience and attributed a

magical virtue to the printed word. In a church
with clear windows the worshipers could read their
Bibles and prayer books and were not tempted to
escape from the sermon into the Other World. On
the Catholic side the men of the Counter Reformation found themselves in two minds. They thought
visionary experience was a good thing, but they also
believed in the supreme value of print.

In the new churches stained glass was rarely installed, and in many of the older churches it was
wholly or partially replaced by clear glass. The un-
obscured light permitted the faithful to follow the
service in their books, and at the same time to see
the vision-inducing works created by the new generations of baroque sculptors and architects. These
transporting works were executed in metal and
polished stone. Wherever the worshiper turned, he
found the glint of bronze, the rich radiance of colored marble, the unearthly whiteness of statuary.

On the rare occasions when the Counter Reform-
ers made use of glass, it was as a surrogate for dia-
monds, not for rubies or sapphires. Faceted prisms
entered religious art in the seventeenth century,
and in Catholic churches they dangle to this day
from innumerable chandeliers. (These charming
and slightly ridiculous ornaments are among the
very few vision-inducing devices permitted in Islam. Mosques have no images or reliquaries; but in
the Near East, at any rate, their austerity is sometimes mitigated by the transporting glitter of ro-
coco crystal.)

From glass, stained or cut, we pass to marble and the other stones that take a high polish and can be used in mass. The fascination exercised by such stones may be gauged by the amount of time and trouble spent in obtaining them. At Baalbek, for example, and, two or three hundred miles further inland, at Palmyra, we find among the ruins columns of pink granite from Aswan. These great monoliths were quarried in Upper Egypt, were floated in barges down the Nile, were towed across the Mediterranean to Byblos or Tripolis and from thence were hauled, by oxen, mules and men, uphill to Homs, and from Homs southward to Baalbek, or east, across the desert, to Palmyra.

What a labor of giants! And, from the utilitarian point of view, how marvelously pointless! But in fact, of course, there was a point—a point that existed in a region beyond mere utility. Polished to a visionary glow, the rosy shafts proclaimed their manifest kinship with the Other World. At the cost of enormous efforts men had transported these stones from their quarry on the Tropic of Cancer; and now, by way of recompense, the stones were transporting their transporters halfway to the mind's visionary antipodes.

The question of utility and of the motives that lie beyond utility arises once more in relation to ceramics. Few things are more useful, more absolutely indispensable, than pots and plates and jugs. But at the same time few human beings concern themselves less with utility than do the collectors of

porcelain and glazed earthenware. To say that
these people have an appetite for beauty is not a
sufficient explanation. The commonplace ugliness
of the surroundings, in which fine ceramics are so
often displayed, is proof enough that what their
owners crave is not beauty in all its manifestations,
but only a special kind of beauty—the beauty of
curved reflections, of softly lustrous glazes, of sleek
and smooth surfaces. In a word, the beauty that
transports the beholder, because it reminds him,
obscurely or explicitly, of the preternatural lights
and colors of the Other World. In the main the art
of the potter has been a secular art—but a secular
art which its innumerable devotees have treated
with an almost idolatrous reverence. From time to
time, however, this secular art has been placed at
the service of religion. Glazed tiles have found their
way into mosques and, here and there, into Christian churches. From China come shining ceramic
images of gods and saints. In Italy Luca della Rob-
bia created a heaven of blue glaze, for his lustrous
white madonnas and Christ children. Baked clay is
cheaper than marble and, suitably treated, almost
as transporting.

Plato and, during a later flowering of religious
art, St. Thomas Aquinas maintained that pure,
bright colors were of the very essence of artistic
beauty. A Matisse, in that case, would be intrinsically superior to a Goya or a Rembrandt. One has
only to translate the philosophers' abstractions into

concrete terms to see that this equation of beauty in general with bright, pure colors is absurd. But though untenable as it stands, the venerable doctrine is not altogether devoid of truth.

Bright, pure colors are characteristic of the Other World. Consequently works of art painted in bright, pure colors are capable, in suitable circumstances, of transporting the beholder's mind in the direction of its antipodes. Bright pure colors are of the essence, not of beauty in general, but only of a special kind of beauty, the visionary. Gothic churches and Greek temples, the statues of the thirteenth century after Christ and of the fifth century before Christ—all were brilliantly colored.

For the Greeks and the men of the Middle Ages, this art of the merry-go-round and the waxwork show was evidently transporting. To us it seems deplorable. We prefer our Praxiteleses plain, our marble and our limestone *au naturel*. Why should our modern taste be so different, in this respect, from that of our ancestors? The reason, I presume, is that we have become too familiar with bright, pure pigments to be greatly moved by them. We admire them, of course, when we see them in some grand or subtle composition; but in themselves and as such, they leave us untransported.

Sentimental lovers of the past complain of the drabness of our age and contrast it unfavorably with the gay brilliance of earlier times. In actual fact, of course, there is a far greater profusion of

color in the modern than in the ancient world.
Lapis lazuli and Tyrian purple were costly rarities;
the rich velvets and brocades of princely wardrobes,
the woven or painted hangings of medieval and
early modern houses were reserved for a privileged
minority.

Even the great ones of the earth possessed very
few of these vision-inducing treasures. As late as
the seventeenth century, monarchs owned so little
furniture that they had to travel from palace to palace with wagonloads of plates and bedspreads, of
carpets and tapestries. For the great mass of the
people there were only homespun and a few vege-
table dyes; and, for interior decoration, there were
at best the earth colors, at worst (and in most cases)
"the floor of plaster and the walls of dung."

At the antipodes of every mind lay the Other
World of preternatural light and preternatural
color, of ideal gems and visionary gold. But before
every pair of eyes was only the dark squalor of the
family hovel, the dust or mud of the village street,
the dirty whites, the duns and goose-turd greens of
ragged clothing. Hence a passionate, an almost des-
perate thirst for bright, pure colors; and hence the
overpowering effect produced by such colors when-
ever, in church or at court, they were displayed.
Today the chemical industry turns out paints, inks
and dyes in endless variety and enormous quantities. In our modern world there is enough bright
color to guarantee the production of billions of flags

and comic strips, millions of stop signs and tail-
lights, fire engines and Coca-Cola containers by the
hundred thousand, carpets, wallpapers and non-
representational art by the square mile.

Familiarity breeds indifference. We have seen too
much pure, bright color at Woolworth's to find it
intrinsically transporting. And here we may note
that, by its amazing capacity to give us too much
of the best things, modern technology has tended
to devaluate the traditional vision-inducing materials. The illumination of a city, for example, was
once a rare event, reserved for victories and national
holidays, for the canonization of saints and the
crowning of kings. Now it occurs nightly and cele-
brates the virtues of gin, cigarettes and toothpaste.

In London, fifty years ago, electric sky signs were
a novelty and so rare that they shone out of the
misty darkness "like captain jewels in the carcanet."
Across the Thames, on the old Shot Tower, the gold
and ruby letters were magically lovely—*une féerie*.
Today the fairies are gone. Neon is everywhere and,
being everywhere, has no effect upon us, except
perhaps to make us pine nostalgically for primeval
night.

Only in floodlighting do we recapture the unearthly significance which used, in the age of oil
and wax, even in the age of gas and the carbon fila-
ment, to shine forth from practically any island of
brightness in the boundless dark. Under the searchlights Notre Dame de Paris and the Roman Forum

are visionary objects, having power to transport the
beholder's mind toward the Other World.*

Modern technology has had the same devaluating
effect on glass and polished metal as it has had on
fairy lamps and pure, bright colors. By John of Pat-
mos and his contemporaries walls of glass were con-
ceivable only in the New Jerusalem. Today they are
a feature of every up-to-date office, building and
bungalow. And this glut of glass has been paralleled
by a glut of chrome and nickel, of stainless steel and
aluminum and a host of alloys old and new. Metal
surfaces wink at us in the bathroom, shine from the
kitchen sink, go glittering across country in cars and
streamliners.

Those rich convex reflections, which so fascinated
Rembrandt that he never tired of rendering them
in paint, are now the commonplaces of home and
street and factory. The fine point of seldom pleasure
has been blunted. What was once a needle of visionary delight has now become a piece of disre-
garded linoleum.

I have spoken so far only of vision-inducing
materials and their psychological devaluation by
modern technology. It is time now to consider the
purely artistic devices, by means of which vision-
inducing works have been created.

Light and color tend to take on a preternatural
quality when seen in the midst of environing darkness. Fra Angelico's "Crucifixion" at the Louvre has
a black background. So have the frescoes of the

* See Appendix III, page 65.

Passion painted by Andrea del Castagno for the nuns of Sant' Appollonia at Florence. Hence the visionary intensity, the strange transporting power of these extraordinary works. In an entirely different artistic and psychological context the same device was often used by Goya in his etchings. Those flying men, that horse on the tightrope, the huge and ghastly incarnation of Fear—all of them stand out, as though floodlit, against a background of impenetrable night.

With the development of chiaroscuro, in the sixteenth and seventeenth centuries, night came out of the background and installed itself within the picture, which became the scene of a kind of Manichean struggle between Light and Darkness. At the time they were painted these works must have possessed a real transporting power. To us, who have seen altogether too much of this kind of thing, most of them seem merely theatrical. But a few still retain their magic. There is Caravaggio's "Entombment," for example; there are a dozen magical paintings by Georges de Latour;* there are all those visionary Rembrandts where the lights have the intensity and significance of light at the mind's antipodes, where the darks are full of rich potentialities waiting their turn to become actual, to make themselves glowingly present to our consciousness.

In most cases the ostensible subject matter of Rembrandt's pictures is taken from real life or the Bible—a boy at his lessons or Bathsheba bathing; a

* See Appendix IV, page 79.

woman wading in a pond or Christ before His
judges. Occasionally, however, these messages from
the Other World are transmitted by means of a subject drawn, not from real life or history, but from
the realm of archetypal symbols. There hangs in
the Louvre a "Meditation du Philosophe," whose
symbolical subject matter is nothing more nor less
than the human mind, with its teeming darknesses,
its moments of intellectual and visionary illumination, its mysterious stairways winding downward
and upward into the unknown. The meditating
philosopher sits there in his island of inner illumination; and at the opposite end of the symbolic
chamber, in another, rosier island, an old woman
crouches before the hearth. The firelight touches
and transfigures her face, and we see, concretely
illustrated, the impossible paradox and supreme
truth—that perception is (or at least can be, ought
to be) the same as Revelation, that Reality shines
out of every appearance, that the One is totally, infinitely present in all particulars.

Along with the preternatural lights and colors,
the gems and the ever-changing patterns, visitors to
the mind's antipodes discover a world of sublimely
beautiful landscapes, of living architecture and of
heroic figures. The transporting power of many
works of art is attributable to the fact that their
creators have painted scenes, persons and objects
which remind the beholder of what, consciously or
unconsciously, he knows about the Other World at
the back of his mind.

Let us begin with the human or, rather, the more than human inhabitants of these far-off regions. Blake called them the Cherubim. And in effect that is what, no doubt, they are—the psychological originals of those beings who, in the theology of every religion, serve as intermediaries between man and the Clear Light. The more than human personages of visionary experience never "do anything." (Similarly the blessed never "do anything" in heaven.) They are content merely to exist.

Under many names and attired in an endless variety of costumes, these heroic figures of man's visionary experience have appeared in the religious art of every culture. Sometimes they are shown at rest, sometimes in historical or mythological action. But action, as we have seen, does not come naturally to the inhabitants of the mind's antipodes. To be busy is the law of *our* being. The law of *theirs* is to do nothing. When we force these serene strangers to play a part in one of our all too human dramas, we are being false to visionary truth. That is why the most transporting (though not necessarily the most beautiful) representation of "the Cherubim" are those which show them as they are in their native habitat—doing nothing in particular.

And that accounts for the overwhelming, the more than merely aesthetic impression made upon the beholder by the great static masterpieces of religious art. The sculptured figures of Egyptian gods and god-kings, the Madonnas and Pantocrators of the Byzantine mosaics, the bodhisattvas, and lohans of China, the seated Buddhas of Khmer, the steles and statues of Copán, the wooden idols of tropical Africa—these have one characteristic in common: a profound stillness. And it is precisely this which gives them their numinous quality, their power to transport the beholder out of the old world of his everyday experience, far away, toward the visionary antipodes of the human psyche.

There is, of course, nothing intrinsically excellent about static art. Static or dynamic, a bad piece of work is always a bad piece of work. All I mean to imply is that, other things being equal, a heroic figure at rest has a greater transporting power than one which is shown in action.

The Cherubim live in Paradise and the New Jerusalem—in other words, among prodigious buildings set in rich, bright gardens with distant prospects of plain and mountain, of rivers and the sea. This is a matter of immediate experience, a psychological fact which has been recorded in folklore and the religious literature of every age and country. It has not, however, been recorded in pictorial art.

Reviewing the succession of human cultures, we find that landscape painting is either non-existent, or rudimentary, or of very recent development. In Europe a full-blown art of landscape painting has existed for only four or five centuries, in China for not more than a thousand years, in India, for all practical purposes, never.

This is a curious fact that demands an explanation. Why should landscapes have found their way into the visionary literature of a given epoch and a given culture, but not into the painting? Posed in this way, the question provides its own best answer. People may be content with the merely verbal expression of this aspect of their visionary experience and feel no need for its translation into pictorial terms.

That this often happens in the case of individuals is certain. Blake, for example, saw visionary landscapes "articulated beyond all that the mortal and perishing nature can produce" and "infinitely more perfect and minutely organized than anything seen by the mortal eye." Here is the description of such a visionary landscape, which Blake gave at one of Mrs. Aders' evening parties: "The other evening, taking a walk, I came to a meadow and at the further corner of it I saw a fold of lambs. Coming nearer, the ground blushed with flowers, and the wattled cote and its woolly tenants were of an exquisite pastoral beauty. But I looked again, and it proved to be no living flock, but beautiful sculpture."

Rendered in pigments, this vision would look, I suppose, like some impossibly beautiful blending of one of Constable's freshest oil sketches with an animal painting in the magically realistic style of Zurbarán's haloed lamb now in the San Diego Museum. But Blake never produced anything remotely

resembling such a picture. He was content to talk
and write about his landscape visions, and to con-
centrate in his painting upon "the Cherubim."

What is true of an individual artist may be true
of a whole school. There are plenty of things which
men experience, but do not choose to express; or
they may try to express what they have experienced,
but in only one of their arts. In yet other cases they
will express themselves in ways having no immediately recognizable affinity to the original experience. In this last context Dr. A. K. Coomaraswamy
has some interesting things to say about the mystical art of the Far East—the art where "denotation
and connotation cannot be divided" and "no dis-
tinction is felt between what a thing 'is' and what it
'signifies.'"

The supreme example of such mystical art is the
Zen-inspired landscape painting which arose in
China during the Sung period and came to new
birth in Japan four centuries later. India and the
Near East have no mystical landscape painting; but
they have its equivalents—"Vaisnava painting, poetry and music in India, where the theme is sexual
love; and Sufi poetry and music in Persia, devoted
to praises of intoxication" *

"Bed," as the Italian proverb succinctly puts it,
"is the poor man's opera." Analogously, sex is the
Hindu's Sung; wine, the Persian's Impressionism.
The reason being, of course, that the experiences of

* A. K. Coomaraswamy, *The Transformation of Nature in
Art*, p. 40.

sexual union and intoxication partake of that essential otherness characteristic of all vision, including that of landscapes.

If, at any time, men have found satisfaction in a certain kind of activity, it is to be presumed that, at periods when this satisfying activity was not manifested, there must have been some kind of equivalent for it. In the Middle Ages, for example, men were preoccupied in an obsessive, an almost maniacal way with words and symbols. Everything in nature was instantly recognized as the concrete illustration of some notion formulated in one of the books or legends currently regarded as sacred.

And yet, at other periods of history men have found a deep satisfaction in recognizing the autonomous otherness of nature, including many aspects of human nature. The experience of this otherness was expressed in terms of art, religion or science. What were the medieval equivalents of Constable and ecology, of bird watching and Eleusis, of microscopy and the rites of Dionysus and the Japanese Haiku? They were to be found, I suspect, in Saturnalian orgies at one end of the scale and in mystical experience at the other. Shrovetides, May Days, Carnivals—these permitted a direct experience of the animal otherness underlying personal and social identity. Infused contemplation revealed the yet otherer otherness of the divine Not-Self. And somewhere between the two extremes were the experiences of the visionaries and the vision-inducing arts, by means of which it was sought to recapture and

re-create those experiences—the art of the jeweler,
of the maker of stained glass, of the weaver of tapestries, of the painter, poet and musician.

In spite of a natural history that was nothing but
a set of drearily moralistic symbols, in the teeth of a
theology which, instead of regarding words as the
signs of things, treated things and events as the
signs of Biblical or Aristotelian words, our ancestors
remained relatively sane. And they achieved this
feat by periodically escaping from the stifling prison
of their bumptiously rationalistic philosophy, their
anthropomorphic, authoritarian and non-experi-
mental science, their all too articulate religion, into
non-verbal, other than human worlds inhabited by
their instincts, by the visionary fauna of their mind's
antipodes and, beyond and yet within all the rest,
by the indwelling Spirit.

From this wide-ranging but necessary digression,
let us return to the particular case from which we
set out. Landscapes, as we have seen, are a regular
feature of the visionary experience. Descriptions of
visionary landscapes occur in the ancient literature
of folklore and religion; but paintings of landscapes
do not make their appearance until comparatively
recent times. To what has been said, by way of explanation about psychological equivalents, I will
add a few brief notes on the nature of landscape
painting as a vision-inducing art.

Let us begin by asking a question. What landscapes—or, more generally, what representations of
natural objects—are most transporting, most in-

trinsically vision inducing? In the light of my own
experience and of what I have heard other people
say about their reactions to works of art, I will risk
an answer. Other things being equal (for nothing
can make up for lack of talent), the most transporting landscapes are, first, those which represent natural objects a very long way off, and, second, those
which represent them at close range.

Distance lends enchantment to the view; but so
does propinquity. A Sung painting of faraway
mountains, clouds and torrents is transporting; but
so are the close-ups of tropical leaves in the Dou-
anier Rousseau's jungles. When I look at the Sung
landscape, I am reminded (or one of my not-I's is
reminded) of the crags, the boundless expanses of
plain, the luminous skies and seas of the mind's antipodes. And those disappearances into mist and
cloud, those sudden emergences of some strange,
intensely definite form, a weathered rock, for example, an ancient pine tree twisted by years of
struggle with the wind—these too, are transporting.
For they remind me, consciously or unconsciously,
of the Other World's essential alienness and unac-
countability.

It is the same with the close-up. I look at those
leaves with their architecture of veins, their stripes
and mottlings, I peer into the depths of interlacing
greenery, and something in me is reminded of those
living patterns, so characteristic of the visionary
world, of those endless births and proliferations of
geometrical forms that turn into objects, of things

that are forever being transmuted into other things.

This painted close-up of a jungle is what, in one
of its aspects, the Other World is like, and so it
transports me, it makes me see with eyes that trans-
figure a work of art into something else, something
beyond art.

I remember—very vividly, though it took place
many years ago—a conversation with Roger Fry.
We were talking about Monet's "Water Lilies."
They had no right, Roger kept insisting, to be so
shockingly unorganized, so totally without a proper
compositional skeleton. They were all wrong, artistically speaking. And yet, he had to admit, and
yet. . . . And yet, as I should now say, they were
transporting. An artist of astounding virtuosity had
chosen to paint a close-up of natural objects seen in
their own context and without reference to merely
human notions of what's what, or what ought to be
what. Man, we like to say, is the measure of all
things. For Monet, on this occasion, water lilies were
the measure of water lilies; and so he painted them.

The same non-human point of view must be
adopted by any artist who tries to render the distant
scene. How tiny, in the Chinese painting, are the
travelers who make their way along the valley! How
frail the bamboo hut on the slope above them! And
all the rest of the vast landscape is emptiness and
silence. This revelation of the wilderness, living its
own life according to the laws of its own being,
transports the mind toward its antipodes; for primeval Nature bears a strange resemblance to that in-

ner world where no account is taken of our personal
wishes or even of the enduring concerns of man in
general.

Only the middle distance and what may be called
the remoter foreground are strictly human. When
we look very near or very far, man either vanishes
altogether or loses his primacy. The astronomer
looks even further afield than the Sung painter and
sees even less of human life. At the other end of the
scale the physicist, the chemist, the physiologist pur-
sue the close-up—the cellular close-up, the mol-
ecular, the atomic and sub-atomic. Of that which,
at twenty feet, even at arm's length, looked and
sounded like a human being no trace remains.

Something analogous happens to the myopic artist and the happy lover. In the nuptial embrace personality is melted down; the individual (it is the
recurrent theme of Lawrence's poems and novels)
ceases to be himself and becomes a part of the vast
impersonal universe.

And so it is with the artist who chooses to use his
eyes at the near point. In his work humanity loses
its importance, even disappears completely. Instead
of men and women playing their fantastic tricks before high heaven, we are asked to consider the lilies,
to meditate on the unearthly beauty of "mere
things," when isolated from their utilitarian context
and rendered as they are, in and for themselves. Al-
ternatively (or, at an earlier stage of artistic development, exclusively) the non-human world of the
near point is rendered in patterns. These patterns

are abstracted for the most part from leaves and flowers—the rose, the lotus, the acanthus, palm, papyrus—and are elaborated, with recurrences and variations, into something transportingly reminiscent of the living geometries of the Other World.

Freer and more realistic treatments of Nature at the near point make their appearance at a relatively recent date—but far earlier than those treatments of the distant scene, to which alone (and mistakenly) we give the name of landscape painting. Rome, for example, had its close-up landscapes. The fresco of a garden, which once adorned a room in Livia's villa, is a magnificent example of this form of art.

For theological reasons, Islam had to be content, for the most part, with "arabesques"—luxuriant and (as in visions) continually varying patterns, based upon natural objects seen at the near point. But even in Islam the genuine close-up landscape was not unknown. Nothing can exceed in beauty and in vision-inducing power the mosaics of gardens and buildings in the great Omayyad mosque at Damascus.

In medieval Europe, despite the prevailing mania for turning every datum into a concept, every immediate experience into a mere symbol of something in a book, realistic close-ups of foliage and flowers were fairly common. We find them carved on the capitals of Gothic pillars, as in the Chapter House of Southwell Cathedral. We find them in paintings of the chase—paintings whose subject was that ever-present fact of medieval life, the forest, seen as the

hunter or the strayed traveler sees it, in all its be-
wildering intricacy of leafy detail.

The frescoes in the papal palace at Avignon are
almost the sole survivors of what, even in the time
of Chaucer, was a widely practiced form of secular
art. A century later this art of the forest close-up
came to its self-conscious perfection in such magnificent and magical works as Pisanello's "St. Hubert"
and Paolo Uccello's "Hunt in a Wood," now in the
Ashmolean Museum at Oxford. Closely related to
the wall paintings of forest close-ups were the tapestries, with which the rich men of northern Europe
adorned their houses. The best of these are vision-
inducing works of the highest order. In their own
way they are as heavenly, as powerfully reminiscent
of what goes on at the mind's antipodes, as are the
great masterpieces of landscape painting at the far-
thest point—Sung mountains in their enormous solitude, Ming rivers interminably lovely, the blue sub-
Alpine world of Titian's distances, the England of
Constable; the Italies of Turner and Corot; the Pro-
vences of Cézanne and Van Gogh; the Île de France
of Sisley and the Île de France of Vuillard.

Vuillard, incidentally, was a supreme master both
of the transporting close-up and of the transporting
distant view. His bourgeois interiors are masterpieces of vision-inducing art, compared with which
the works of such conscious and so to say profes-
sional visionaries as Blake and Odilon Redon seem
feeble in the extreme. In Vuillard's interior every
detail however trivial, however hideous even—the

pattern of the late Victorian wallpaper, the *art nouveau* bibelot, the Brussels carpet—is seen and rendered as a living jewel; and all these jewels are harmoniously combined into a whole which is a jewel of a yet higher order of visionary intensity. And when the upper middle-class inhabitants of Vuillard's New Jerusalem go for a walk, they find themselves not, as they had supposed, in the department of Seine-et-Oise, but in the Garden of Eden, in an Other World which is yet essentially the same as this world, but transfigured and therefore transporting.*

I have spoken so far only of the blissful visionary experience and of its interpretation in terms of theology, its translation into art. But visionary experience is not always blissful. It is sometimes terrible. There is hell as well as heaven.

Like heaven, the visionary hell has its preternatural light and its preternatural significance. But the significance is intrinsically appalling and the light is "the smoky light" of the *Tibetan Book of the Dead*, the "darkness visible" of Milton. In the *Journal d'une Schizophrène*,† the autobiographical record of a young girl's passage through madness, the world of the schizophrenic is called *le Pays d'Éclairement*—"the country of lit-upness." Is is a name which a mystic might have used to denote his heaven. But for poor Renée, the schizophrenic, the illumination is infernal—an intense electric glare without a shadow,

---

* See Appendix V, page 82.

† *Journal d'une Schizophrène*, by M. A. Sechehaye. Paris, 1950.

ubiquitous and implacable. Everything that, for healthy visionaries, is a source of bliss brings to Renée only fear and a nightmarish sense of unreality. The summer sunshine is malignant; the gleam of polished surfaces is suggestive not of gems, but of machinery and enameled tin; the intensity of existence which animates every object, when seen at close range and out of its utilitarian context, is felt as a menace.

And then there is the horror of infinity. For the healthy visionary, the perception of the infinite in a finite particular is a revelation of divine immanence; for Renée, it was a revelation of what she calls "the System," the vast cosmic mechanism which exists only to grind out guilt and punishment, solitude and unreality.*

Sanity is a matter of degree, and there are plenty of visionaries, who see the world as Renée saw it, but contrive, none the less, to live outside the asylum. For them, as for the positive visionary, the universe is transfigured—but for the worse. Everything in it, from the stars in the sky to the dust under their feet, is unspeakably sinister or disgusting; every event is charged with a hateful significance; every object manifests the presence of an Indwelling Horror, infinite, all-powerful, eternal.

This negatively transfigured world has found its way, from time to time, into literature and the arts. It writhed and threatened in Van Gogh's later landscapes; it was the setting and the theme of all Kaf-

* See Appendix VI, page 86.

ka's stories; it was Géricault's spiritual home;° it was inhabited by Goya during the long years of his deafness and solitude; it was glimpsed by Browning when he wrote *Childe Roland;* it had its place, over against the theophanies, in the novels of Charles Williams.

The negative visionary experience is often accompanied by bodily sensations of a very special and characteristic kind. Blissful visions are generally associated with a sense of separation from the body, a feeling of deindividualization. (It is, no doubt, this feeling of deindividualization which makes it possible for the Indians who practice the peyote cult to use the drug not merely as a short cut to the visionary world, but also as an instrument for creating a loving solidarity within the participating group.) When the visionary experience is terrible and the world is transfigured for the worse, individualization is intensified and the negative visionary finds himself associated with a body that seems to grow progressively more dense, more tightly packed, until he finds himself at last reduced to being the agonized consciousness of an inspissated lump of matter, no bigger than a stone that can be held between the hands.

It is worth remarking, that many of the punishments described in the various accounts of hell are punishments of pressure and constriction. Dante's sinners are buried in mud, shut up in the trunks of trees, frozen solid in blocks of ice, crushed beneath

° See Appendix VII, page 88.

stones. The *Inferno* is psychologically true. Many of its pains are experienced by schizophrenics, and by those who have taken mescalin or lysergic acid under unfavorable conditions.*

What is the nature of these unfavorable conditions? How and why is heaven turned into hell? In certain cases the negative visionary experience is the result of predominantly physical causes. Mescalin tends, after ingestion, to accumulate in the liver. If the liver is diseased, the associated mind may find itself in hell. But what is more important for our present purposes is the fact that negative visionary experience may be induced by purely psychological means. Fear and anger bar the way to the heavenly Other World and plunge the mescalin taker into hell.

And what is true of the mescalin taker is also true of the person who sees visions spontaneously or under hypnosis. Upon this psychological foundation has been reared the theological doctrine of saving faith—a doctrine to be met with in all the great religious traditions of the world. Eschatologists have always found it difficult to reconcile their rationality and their morality with the brute facts of psychological experience. As rationalists and moralists, they feel that good behavior should be rewarded and that the virtuous deserve to go to heaven. But as psychologists they know that virtue is not the sole or sufficient condition of blissful visionary experience. They know that works alone are powerless

* See Appendix VIII, page 90.

and that it is faith, or loving confidence, which guarantees that visionary experience shall be blissful.

Negative emotions—the fear which is the absence of confidence, the hatred, anger or malice which exclude love—are the guarantee that visionary experience, if and when it comes, shall be appalling. The Pharisee is a virtuous man; but his virtue is of the kind which is compatible with negative emotion. His visionary experiences are therefore likely to be infernal rather than blissful.

The nature of the mind is such that the sinner who repents and makes an act of faith in a higher power is more likely to have a blissful visionary experience than is the self-satisfied pillar of society with his righteous indignations, his anxiety about possessions and pretensions, his ingrained habits of blaming, despising and condemning. Hence the enormous importance attached, in all the great religious traditions, to the state of mind at the moment of death.

Visionary experience is not the same as mystical experience. Mystical experience is beyond the realm of opposites. Visionary experience is still within that realm. Heaven entails hell, and "going to heaven" is no more liberation than is the descent into horror. Heaven is merely a vantage point, from which the divine Ground can be more clearly seen than on the level of ordinary individualized existence.

If consciousness survives bodily death, it survives, presumably, on every mental level—on the level of mystical experience, on the level of blissful visionary

experience, on the level of infernal visionary experience, and on the level of everyday individual existence. In life, as we know by experience and observation, even the blissful visionary experience tends
to change its sign if it persists too long.

Many schizophrenics have their times of heavenly
happiness; but the fact that (unlike the mescalin
taker) they do not know when, if ever, they will be
permitted to return to the reassuring banality of
everyday experience causes even heaven to seem
appalling. But for those who, for whatever reason,
are appalled, heaven turns into hell, bliss into horror, the Clear Light into the hateful glare of the land
of lit-upness.

Something of the same kind may happen in the
posthumous state. After having had a glimpse of the
unbearable splendor of ultimate Reality, and after
having shuttled back and forth between heaven and
hell, most souls find it possible to retreat into that
more reassuring region of the mind, where they can
use their own and other people's wishes, memories
and fancies to construct a world very like that in
which they lived on earth.

Of those who die an infinitesimal minority are
capable of immediate union with the divine Ground,
a few are capable of supporting the visionary bliss
of heaven, a few find themselves in the visionary
horrors of hell and are unable to escape; the great
majority end up in the kind of world described by
Swedenborg and the mediums. From this world it
is doubtless possible to pass, when the necessary

conditions have been fulfilled, to worlds of visionary bliss or the final enlightenment.

My own guess is that modern spiritualism and ancient tradition are both correct. There *is* a posthumous state of the kind described in Sir Oliver Lodge's book *Raymond;* but there is also a heaven of blissful visionary experience; there is also a hell of the same kind of appalling visionary experience as is suffered here by schizophrenics and some of those who take mescalin; and there is also an experience, beyond time, of union with the divine Ground.

APPENDICES

I

Two other, less effective aids to visionary experience deserve mention—carbon dioxide and the stroboscopic lamp. A mixture (completely non-toxic) of seven parts of oxygen and three of carbon dioxide produces, in those who inhale it, certain physical and psychological changes, which have been exhaustively described by Meduna. Among these changes the most important, in our present context, is a marked enhancement of the ability to "see things," when the eyes are closed. In some cases only swirls of patterned color are seen. In others there may be vivid recalls of past experiences. (Hence the value of CO_2 as a therapeutic agent.) In yet other cases carbon dioxide transports the subject to the Other World at the antipodes of his everyday consciousness, and he enjoys very briefly visionary experiences entirely unconnected with his own personal history or with the problems of the human race in general.

In the light of these facts it becomes easy to understand the rationale of yogic breathing exercises.

Practiced systematically, these exercises result, after a time, in prolonged suspensions of breath. Long suspensions of breath lead to a high concentration of carbon dioxide in the lungs and blood, and this increase in the concentration of CO_2 lowers the efficiency of the brain as a reducing value and permits the entry into consciousness of experiences, visionary or mystical, from "out there."

Prolonged and continuous shouting or singing may produce similar, but less strongly marked, results. Unless they are highly trained, singers tend to breathe out more than they breathe in. Consequently the concentration of carbon dioxide in the alveolar air and the blood is increased and, the efficiency of the cerebral reducing valve being lowered, visionary experience becomes possible. Hence the interminable "vain repetitions" of magic and religion. The chanting of the *curandero,* the medicine man, the shaman; the endless psalm singing and sutra intoning of Christian and Buddhist monks; the shouting and howling, hour after hour, of revivalists —under all the diversities of theological belief and aesthetic convention, the psychochemico-physiological intention remains constant. To increase the concentration of CO_2 in the lungs and blood and so to lower the efficiency of the cerebral reducing valve, until it will admit biologically useless material from Mind-at-Large—this, though the shouters, singers and mutterers did not know it, has been at all times the real purpose and point of magic spells, of mantrams, litanies, psalms and sutras.

"The heart," said Pascal, "has its reasons." Still more cogent and much harder to unravel are the reasons of the lungs, the blood and the enzymes, of neurons and synapses. The way to the superconscious is through the subconscious, and the way, or at least one of the ways, to the subconscious is through the chemistry of individual cells.

With the stroboscopic lamp we descend from chemistry to the still more elementary realm of physics. Its rhythmically flashing light seems to act directly, through the optic nerves, on the electrical manifestations of the brain's activity. (For this reason there is always a slight danger involved in the use of the stroboscopic lamp. Some persons suffer from *petit mal* without being made aware of the fact by any clear-cut and unmistakable symptoms. Exposed to a stroboscopic lamp, such persons may go into a full-blown epileptic fit. The risk is not very great; but it must always be recognized. One case in eighty may turn out badly.)

To sit, with eyes closed, in front of a stroboscopic lamp is a very curious and fascinating experience. No sooner is the lamp turned on than the most brilliantly colored patterns make themselves visible. These patterns are not static, but change incessantly. Their prevailing color is a function of the stroboscope's rate of discharge. When the lamp is flashing at any speed between ten to fourteen or fifteen times a second, the patterns are prevailingly orange and red. Green and blue make their appearance when the rate exceeds fifteen flashes a second.

After eighteen or nineteen, the patterns become
white and gray. Precisely why we should see such
patterns under the stroboscope is not known. The
most obvious explanation would be in terms of the
interference of two or more rhythms—the rhythm
of the lamp and the various rhythms of the brain's
electrical activity. Such interferences may be translated by the visual center and optic nerves into
something of which the mind becomes conscious as
a colored, moving pattern. Far more difficult to explain is the fact, independently observed by several
experimenters, that the stroboscope tends to enrich
and intensify the visions induced by mescalin or
lysergic acid. Here, for example, is a case communi-
cated to me by a medical friend. He had taken lysergic acid and was seeing, with his eyes shut, only
colored, moving patterns. Then he sat down in front
of a stroboscope. The lamp was turned on and, immediately, abstract geometry was transformed into
what my friend described as "Japanese landscapes"
of surpassing beauty. But how on earth can the interference of two rhythms produce an arrangement
of electrical impulses interpretable as a living, self-
modulating Japanese landscape unlike anything the
subject has ever seen, suffused with preternatural
light and color and charged with preternatural significance?

This mystery is merely a particular case of a
larger, more comprehensive mystery—the nature of
the relations between visionary experience and
events on the cellular, chemical and electrical levels.

By touching certain areas of the brain with a very fine electrode, Penfield has been able to induce the recall of a long chain of memories relating to some past experience. This recall is not merely accurate in every perceptual detail; it is also accompanied by all the emotions which were aroused by the events when they originally occurred. The patient, who is under a local anesthetic, finds himself simultaneously in two times and places—in the operating room, now, and in his childhood home, hundreds of miles away and thousands of days in the past. Is there, one wonders, some area in the brain from which the probing electrode could elicit Blake's Cherubim, or Weir Mitchell's self-transformating Gothic tower encrusted with living gems, or my friend's unspeakably lovely Japanese landscapes? And if, as I myself believe, visionary experiences enter our consciousness from somewhere "out there" in the infinity of Mind-at-Large, what sort of an *ad hoc* neurological pattern is created for them by the receiving and transmitting brain? And what happens to this *ad hoc* pattern when the vision is over? Why do all visionaries insist on the impossibility of recalling, in anything even faintly resembling its original form and intensity, their transfiguring experiences? How many questions—and, as yet, how few answers!

II

In the Western world, visionaries and mystics are a good deal less common than they used to be. There are two principal reasons for this state of affairs—a philosophical reason and a chemical reason. In the currently fashionable picture of the universe there is no place for valid transcendental experience. Consequently those who have had what they regard as valid transcendental experiences are looked upon with suspicion as being either lunatics or swindlers. To be a mystic or a visionary is no longer creditable.

But it is not only our mental climate that is unfavorable to the visionary and the mystic; it is also our chemical environment—an environment profoundly different from that in which our forefathers passed their lives.

The brain is chemically controlled, and experience has shown that it can be made permeable to the (biologically speaking) superfluous aspects of Mind-at-Large by modifying the (biologically speaking) normal chemistry of the body.

For almost half of every year our ancestors ate no

fruit, no green vegetables and (since it was impossible for them to feed more than a few oxen, cows, swine and poultry during the winter months) very little butter or fresh meat, and very few eggs. By the beginning of each successive spring, most of them were suffering, mildly or acutely, from scurvy, due to lack of Vitamin C, and pellagra, caused by a shortage in their diet of the B complex. The distressing physical symptoms of these diseases are associated with no less distressing psychological symptoms.* The nervous system is more vulnerable than the other tissues of the body; consequently vitamin deficiencies tend to affect the state of mind before they affect, at least in any very obvious way, the skin, bones, mucous membranes, muscles and viscera. The first result of an inadequate diet is a lowering of the efficiency of the brain as an instrument for biological survival. The undernourished person tends to be afflicted by anxiety, depression, hypochondria and feelings of anxiety. He is also liable to see visions; for when the cerebral reducing valve has its efficiency lowered, much (biologically speaking) useless material flows into consciousness from "out there," in Mind-at-Large.

Much of what the earlier visionaries experienced was terrifying. To use the language of Christian theology, the Devil revealed himself in their visions

---

* See *The Biology of Human Starvation* by A. Keys (University of Minnesota Press, 1950); also the recent (1955) reports of the work on the role of vitamin deficiencies in mental disease, carried out by Dr. George Watson and his associates in Southern California.

and ecstasies a good deal more frequently than did
God. In an age when vitamins were deficient and
a belief in Satan universal, this was not surprising.
The mental distress, associated with even mild cases
of pellagra and scurvy, was deepened by fears of
damnation and a conviction that the powers of evil
were omnipresent. This distress was apt to tinge
with its own dark coloring the visionary material,
admitted to consciousness through a cerebral valve
whose efficiency had been impaired by underfeed-
ing. But in spite of their preoccupations with eternal
punishment and in spite of their deficiency disease,
spiritually minded ascetics often saw heaven and
might even be aware, occasionally, of that divinely
impartial One in which the polar opposites are re-
conciled. For a glimpse of beatitude, for a foretaste
of unitive knowledge, no price seemed too high.
Mortification of the body may produce a host of
undesirable mental symptoms; but it may also open
a door into a transcendental world of Being, Knowledge and Bliss. That is why, in spite of its obvious
disadvantages, almost all aspirants to the spiritual
life have, in the past, undertaken regular courses of
bodily mortification.

So far as vitamins were concerned, every medieval winter was a long involuntary fast, and this involuntary fast was followed, during Lent, by forty
days of voluntary abstinence. Holy Week found the
faithful marvelously well prepared, so far as their
body chemistry was concerned, for its tremendous
incitements to grief and joy, for seasonable remorse

of conscious and a self-transcending identification
with the risen Christ. At this season of the highest
religious excitement and the lowest vitamin intake,
ecstasies and visions were almost a commonplace. It
was only to be expected.

For cloistered contemplatives, there were several
Lents in every year. And even between fasts their
diet was meager in the extreme. Hence those agonies
of depression and scrupulosity described by so
many spiritual writers; hence their frightful temptations to despair and self-slaughter. But hence too
those "gratuitous graces" in the form of heavenly
visions and locutions, of prophetic insights, of tele-
pathic "discernments of spirits." And hence, finally,
their "infused contemplation," their "obscure knowledge" of the One in all.

Fasting was not the only form of physical mortification resorted to by the earlier aspirants to spiritu-
ality. Most of them regularly used upon themselves
the whip of knotted leather or even of iron wire.
These beatings were the equivalent of fairly exten-
sive surgery without anesthetics, and their effects
on the body chemistry of the penitent were consid-
erable. Large quantities of histamine and adrenalin
were released while the whip was actually being
plied; and when the resulting wounds began to
fester (as wounds practically always did before the
age of soap), various toxic substances, produced by
the decomposition of protein, found their way into
the blood stream. But histamine produces shock,
and shock affects the mind no less profoundly than

the body. Moreover, large quantities of adrenalin
may cause hallucinations, and some of the products
of its decomposition are known to induce symptoms
resembling those of schizophrenia. As for toxins
from wounds—these upset the enzyme systems reg-
ulating the brain, and lower its efficiency as an
instrument for getting on in a world where the biologically fittest survive. This may explain why the
Curé d'Ars used to say that, in the days when he was
free to flagellate himself without mercy, God would
refuse him nothing. In other words, when remorse,
self-loathing and the fear of hell release adrenalin,
when self-inflicted surgery releases adrenalin and
histamine, and when infected wounds release decomposed protein into the blood, the efficiency of
the cerebral reducing valve is lowered and unfamiliar aspects of Mind-at-Large (including psi
phenomena, visions and, if he is philosophically and
ethically prepared for it, mystical experiences) will
flow into the ascetic's consciousness.

Lent, as we have seen, followed a long period of
involuntary fasting. Analogously, the effects of self-
flagellation were supplemented, in earlier times, by
much involuntary absorption of decomposed protein. Dentistry was non-existent, surgeons were ex-
ecutioners, and there were no safe antiseptics. Most
people, therefore, must have lived out their lives
with focal infections; and focal infections, though
out of fashion as the cause of *all* the ills that flesh is
heir to, can certainly lower the efficiency of the
cerebral reducing valve.

And the moral of all this is—what? Exponents of a Nothing-But philosophy will answer that, since changes in body chemistry can create the conditions favorable to visionary and mystical experiences, visionary and mystical experiences cannot be what they claim to be, what, for those who have had them, they self-evidently are. But this, of course, is a *non sequitur*.

A similar conclusion will be reached by those whose philosophy is unduly "spiritual." God, they will insist, is a spirit and is to be worshiped in spirit. Therefore an experience which is chemically conditioned cannot be an experience of the divine. But, in one way or another, *all* our experiences are chemically conditioned, and if we imagine that some of them are purely "spiritual," purely "intellectual," purely "aesthetic," it is merely because we have never troubled to investigate the internal chemical environment at the moment of their occurrence. Furthermore, it is a matter of historical record that most contemplatives worked systematically to modify their body chemistry, with a view to creating the internal conditions favorable to spiritual insight. When they were not starving themselves into low blood sugar and a vitamin deficiency, or beating themselves into intoxication by histamine, adrenalin and decomposed protein, they were cultivating insomnia and praying for long periods in uncomfortable positions in order to create the psycho-physical symptoms of stress. In the intervals they sang interminable psalms, thus increasing the amount of carbon dioxide in the lungs and the blood stream, or, if they were Orientals, they did breathing exercises to accomplish the same purpose. Today we know how to lower the efficiency of the cerebral reducing valve by direct chemical action, and without the risk of inflicting serious damage on the psychophysical organism. For an aspiring mystic to revert, in the present state of knowledge, to prolonged fasting and violent self-flagellation would be as senseless as it would be for an aspiring cook to behave like Charles Lamb's Chinaman, who burned down the house in order to roast a pig. Knowing as he does (or at least as he can know, if he so desires) what are the chemical conditions of transcendental experience, the aspiring mystic should turn for technical help to the specialists—in pharmacology, in biochemistry, in physiology and neurology, in psychology and psychiatry, and parapsychology. And on their part, of course, the specialists (if any of them aspire to be genuine men of science and complete human beings) should turn, out of their respective pigeonholes, to the artist, the sibyl, the visionary, the mystic—all those, in a word, who have had experience of the Other World and who know, in their different ways, what to do with that experience.

III

Visionlike effects and vision-inducing devices have
played a greater part in popular entertainment
than in the fine arts. Fireworks, pageantry, theatrical spectacles—those are essentially visionary
arts. Unfortunately they are also ephemeral arts,
whose earlier masterpieces are known to us only by
report. Nothing remains of all the Roman triumphs,
the medieval tournaments, the Jacobean masques,
the long succession of state entries and coronations,
of royal marriages and solemn decapitations, of can-
onizations and the funerals of Popes. The best that
can be hoped for such magnificences is that they
may "live in Settle's numbers one day more."

An interesting feature of these popular visionary
arts is their close dependence upon contemporary
technology. Fireworks, for example, were once no
more than bonfires. (And to this day, I may add, a
good bonfire on a dark night remains one of the
most magical and transporting of spectacles. Looking at it, one can understand the mentality of the
Mexican peasant, who sets out to burn an acre of

woodland in order to plant his maize, but is de-
lighted when, by a happy accident, a square mile
or two goes up in bright, apocalyptic flame.) True
pyrotechny began (in Europe at least, if not in
China) with the use of combustibles in sieges and
naval battles. From war it passed, in due course, to
entertainment. Imperial Rome had its firework dis-
plays, some of which, even in its decline, were elaborate in the extreme. Here is Claudian's description
of the show put on by Manlius Theodorus in A.D.
399.

> Mobile ponderibus descendat pegma reductis
> inque chori speciem spargentes ardua flammas
> scaena rotet varios, et fingat Mulciber orbis
> per tabulas impune vagos pictaeque citato
> ludent igne trabes, et non permissa morari
> fida per innocuas errent incendia turres.

"Let the counterweights be removed," Mr. Plat-
nauer translates with a straightforwardness of language that does less than justice to the syntactical
extravagances of the original, "and let the mobile
crane descend, lowering on to the lofty stage men
who, wheeling chorus-wise, scatter flames. Let Vul-
can forge balls of fire to roll innocuously across the
boards. Let the flames appear to play about the
sham beams of the scenery and a tame conflagra-
tion, never allowed to rest, wander among the un-
touched towers."

After the fall of Rome, pyrotechny became, once
more, exclusively a military art. Its greatest triumph

was the invention by Callinicus, about A.D. 650, of the famous Greek Fire—the secret weapon which enabled a dwindling Byzantine Empire to hold out for so long against its enemies.

With the Renaissance, fireworks re-entered the world of popular entertainment. With every advance in the science of chemistry, they became more and more brilliant. By the middle of the nineteenth century pyrotechny had reached a peak of technical perfection and was capable of transporting vast multitudes of spectators toward the visionary antipodes of minds which, consciously, were respectable Methodists, Puseyites, Utilitarians, disciples of Mill or Marx or Newman, or Bradlaugh, or Samuel Smiles. In the Piazza del Popolo, at Ranelagh and the Crystal Palace, on every Fourth and Fourteenth of July, the popular subconscious was reminded by the crimson glare of strontium, by copper blue and barium green and sodium yellow, of that Other World, down under, in the psychological equivalent of Australia.

Pageantry is a visionary art which has been used, from time immemorial, as a political instrument. The gorgeous fancy dress worn by kings, popes and their respective retainers, military and ecclesiastical, has a very practical purpose—to impress the lower classes with a lively sense of their masters' superhuman greatness. By means of fine clothes and solemn ceremonies *de facto* domination is transformed into a rule not merely *de jure*, but, positively, *de jure divino*. The crowns and tiaras, the assorted jew-

elry, the satins, silks and velvets, the gaudy uniforms
and vestments, the crosses and medals, the sword
hilts and the crosiers, the plumes in the cocked hats
and their clerical equivalents, those huge feather
fans which make every papal function look like a
tableau from *Aïda*—all these are vision-inducing
properties, designed to make all too human gentle-
men and ladies look like heroes, demigoddesses and
seraphs, and giving, in the process, a great deal of
innocent pleasure to all concerned, actors and spectators alike.

In the course of the last two hundred years the
technology of artificial lighting has made enormous
progress, and this progress has contributed very
greatly to the effectiveness of pageantry and the
closely related art of theatrical spectacle. The first
notable advance was made in the eighteenth century, with the introduction of molded spermaceti
candles in place of the older tallow dip and poured
wax taper. Next came the invention of Argand's
tubular wick, with an air supply on the inner as well
as the outer surface of the flame. Glass chimneys
speedily followed, and it became possible, for the
first time in history, to burn oil with a bright and
completely smokeless light. Coal gas was first em-
ployed as an illuminant in the early years of the
nineteenth century, and in 1825 Thomas Drummond found a practical way of heating lime to incandescence by means of an oxygen-hydrogen or
oxygen-coal gas flame. Meanwhile parabolic reflectors for concentrating light into a narrow beam had

come into use. (The first English lighthouse
equipped with such a reflector was built in 1790.)

The influence on pageantry and theatrical spectacle of these inventions was profound. In earlier
times civic and religious ceremonies could only take
place during the day (and days were as often cloudy
as fine), or by the light, after sunset, of smoky lamps
and torches or the feeble twinkling of candles. Argand and Drummond, gas, limelight and, forty
years later, electricity made it possible to evoke,
from the boundless chaos of night, rich island uni-
verses, in which the glitter of metal and gems, the
sumptuous glow of velvets and brocades were intensified to the highest pitch of what may be called
intrinsic significance. A recent example of ancient
pageantry, raised by twentieth-century lighting to a
higher magical power, was the coronation of Queen
Elizabeth II. In the motion picture of the event, a
ritual of transporting splendor was saved from the
oblivion, which, up till now, has always been the
fate of such solemnities, and preserved, blazing preternaturally under the floodlights, for the delight of
a vast contemporary and future audience.

Two distinct and separate arts are practiced in
the theater—the human art of the drama and the
visionary, other-world art of spectacle. Elements of
the two arts may be combined in a single evening's
entertainment—the drama being interrupted (as so
often happens in elaborate productions of Shakes-
peare) to permit the audience to enjoy a *tableau
vivant* in which the actors either remain still or, if

they move, move only in a non-dramatic way, cere-
monially, processionally, or in a formal dance. Our
concern here is not with drama; it is with theatrical
spectacle, which is simply pageantry without its
political or religious overtones.

In the minor visionary arts of the costumier and
the designer of stage jewelry our ancestors were con-
summate masters. Nor, for all their dependence on
unassisted muscle power, were they far behind us
in the building and working of stage machinery,
the contrivance of "special effects." In the masques
of Elizabethan and early Stuart times, divine de-
scents and irruptions of demons from the cellarage
were a commonplace, so were apocalypses, so were
the most amazing metamorphoses. Enormous sums
of money were lavished on these spectacles. The
Inns of Court, for example, put on a show for
Charles I, which cost more than twenty thousand
pounds—at a date when the purchasing power of
the pound was six or seven times what it is today.

"Carpentry," said Ben Jonson sarcastically, "is the
soul of masque." His contempt was motivated by re-
sentment. Inigo Jones was paid as much for design-
ing the scenery as was Ben for writing the libretto.
The outraged laureate had evidently failed to grasp
the fact that masque is a visionary art, and that visionary experience is beyond words (at any rate
beyond all but the most Shakespearean words) and
is to be evoked by direct, unmeditated perceptions
of things that remind the beholder of what is going
on at the unexplored antipodes of his own personal

consciousness. The soul of masque could never, in the very nature of things, be a Jonsonian libretto; it *had* to be carpentry. But even carpentry could not be the masque's whole soul. When it comes to us from within, visionary experience is always preternaturally brilliant. But the early set designers possessed no manageable illuminant brighter than a candle. At close range a candle can create the most magical lights and contrasting shadows. The visionary paintings of Rembrandt and Georges de Latour are of things and persons seen by candlelight. Unfortunately light obeys the law of the inverse squares. At a safe distance from an actor in inflammable fancy dress, candles are hopelessly inadequate. At ten feet, for example, it would take one hundred of the best wax tapers to produce an effective illumination of one foot-candle. With such miserable lighting only a fraction of the masque's visionary potentialities could be made actual. Indeed, its visionary potentialities were not fully realized until long after it had ceased, in its original form, to exist. It was only in the nineteenth century, when advancing technology had equipped the theater with limelight and parabolic reflectors, that the masque came fully into its own. Victoria's reign was the heroic age of the so-called Christmas pantomime and the fantastic spectacle. "Ali Baba," "The King of the Peacocks," "The Golden Branch," "The Island of Jewels"—their very names are magical. The soul of that theatrical magic was carpentry and dressmaking; its indwelling spirit, its *scintilla animae*, was gas

and limelight and, after the eighties, electricity. For
the first time in the history of the stage, beams of
brightest incandescence transfigured the painted
backdrops, the costumes, the glass and pinchbeck
of jewelry, so that they became capable of transporting the spectators toward that Other World,
which lies at the back of every mind, however perfect its adaptation to the exigencies of social life—
even the social life of mid-Victorian England. Today we are in the fortunate position of being able to
squander half a million horsepower on the nightly
illumination of a metropolis. And yet, in spite of this
devaluation of artificial light, theatrical spectacle
still retains its old compelling magic. Embodied in
ballets, revues and musical comedies, the soul of
masque goes marching along. Thousand-watt lamps
and parabolic reflectors project beams of preternatural light, and preternatural light evokes, in everything it touches, preternatural color and preternatural significance. Even the silliest spectacle can
be rather wonderful. It is a case of a New World
having been called in to redress the balance of the
Old—of visionary art making up for the deficiencies
of all too human drama.

Athanasius Kircher's invention—if his, indeed, it
was—was christened from the first *Lanterna Mag-
ica*. The name was everywhere adopted as perfectly
appropriate to a machine, whose raw material was
light, and whose finished product was a colored
image emerging from the darkness. To make the
original magic lantern show yet more magical,

Kircher's successors devised a number of methods for imparting life and movement to the projected image. There were "chrometropic" slides in which two painted glass disks could be made to revolve in opposite directions, producing a crude but still effective imitation of those perpetually changing three-dimensional patterns, which have been seen by virtually everyone who has had a vision, whether spontaneous or induced by drugs, fasting or the stroboscopic lamp. Then there were those "dissolving views," which reminded the spectator of the metamorphoses going on incessantly at the antipodes of his everyday consciousness. To make one scene turn imperceptibly into another, two magic lanterns were used, projecting coincident images on the screen. Each lantern was fitted with a shutter, so arranged that the light of one could be progressively dimmed, while the light of the other (originally completely obscured) was progressively brightened. In this way the view projected by the first lantern was insensibly replaced by the view projected by the second—to the delight and astonishment of all beholders. Another device was the mobile magic lantern, projecting its image on a semi-transparent screen, on the further side of which sat the audience. When the lantern was wheeled close to the screen, the projected image was very small. As it was withdrawn, the image became progressively larger. An automatic focusing device kept the changing images sharp and unblurred at all distances. The word "phantasmagoria"

was coined in 1802 by the inventors of this new kind
of peepshow.

All these improvements in the technology of
magic lanterns were contemporary with the poets
and painters of the Romantic revival, and may perhaps have exercised a certain influence on their
choice of subject matter and their methods of treat-
ing it. *Queen Mab* and *The Revolt of Islam,* for example, are full of dissolving views and phantasma-
gorias. Keat's descriptions of scenes and persons, of
interiors and furniture and effects of light have the
intense beamy quality of colored images on a white
sheet in a darkened room. John Martin's representations of Satan and Belshazzar, of Hell and Babylon
and the Deluge are manifestly inspired by lantern
slides and *tableaux vivants* dramatically illuminated
by limelight.

The twentieth-century equivalent of the magic-
lantern show is the colored movie. In the huge, ex-
pensive "spectaculars," the soul of masque goes
marching along—with a vengeance sometimes, but
sometimes also with taste and a real feeling for
vision-inducing fantasy. Moreover, thanks to advancing technology, the colored documentary has
proved itself, in skillful hands, a notable new form
of popular visionary art. The immensely magnified
cactus blossoms, into which, at the end of Disney's
The Living Desert, the spectator finds himself sink-
ing, come straight from the Other World. And then
what transporting visions, in the best of the nature
films, of foliage in the wind, of the textures of rock

and sand, of the shadows and emerald lights in
grass or among the reeds, of birds and insects and
four-footed creatures going about their business in
the underbrush or among the branches of forest
trees! Here are the magical close-up landscapes
which fascinated the makers of *mille-feuille* tapestries, the medieval painters of gardens and hunting
scenes. Here are the enlarged and isolated details of
living nature, out of which the artists of the Far
East made some of the most beautiful of their paintings.

And then there is what may be called the Dis-
torted Documentary—a new form of visionary art,
admirably exemplified by Mr. Francis Thompson's
film, *NY, NY*. In this very strange and beautiful picture we see the city of New York as it appears when
photographed through multiplying prisms, or reflected in the backs of spoons, polished hub caps,
spherical and parabolic mirrors. We still recognize
houses, people, shop fronts, taxicabs, but recognize
them as elements in one of those living geometries
which are so characteristic of the visionary experience. The invention of this new cinematographic art
seems to presage (thank heaven!) the supersession
and early demise of non-representational painting.
It used to be said by the non-representationalists
that colored photography had reduced the old-
fashioned portrait and the old-fashioned landscape
to the rank of otiose absurdities. This, of course, is
completely untrue. Colored photography merely
records and preserves, in an easily reproducible

form, the raw materials with which portraitists and
landscape painters work. Used as Mr. Thompson
has used it, colored cinematography does much
more than merely record and preserve the raw materials of non-representational art; it actually turns
out the finished product. Looking at *NY, NY*, I was
amazed to see that virtually every pictorial device
invented by the old masters of non-representational
art and reproduced *ad nauseam* by the academi-
cians and mannerists of the school, for the last forty
years or more, makes its appearance, alive, glowing,
intensely significant, in the sequences of Mr.
Thompson's film.

Our ability to project a powerful beam of light
has not only enabled us to create new forms of visionary art; it has also endowed one of the most
ancient arts, the art of sculpture, with a new visionary quality which it did not previously possess. I
have spoken in an earlier paragraph of the magical
effects produced by the floodlighting of ancient
monuments and natural objects. Analogous effects
are seen when we turn the spotlights onto sculptured stone. Fuseli got the inspiration for some of
his best and wildest pictorial ideas by studying the
statues on Monte Cavallo by the light of the setting
sun, or, better still, when illuminated by lightning
flashes at midnight. Today we dispose of artificial
sunsets and synthetic lightning. We can illuminate
our statues from whatever angle we choose, and
with practically any desired degree of intensity.
Sculpture, in consequence, has revealed fresh mean-

ings and unsuspected beauties. Visit the Louvre one
night when the Greek and Egyptian antiquities are
floodlit. You will meet with new gods, nymphs and
Pharaohs; you will make the acquaintance, as one
spotlight goes out and another, in a different quarter
of space, is lit up, of a whole family of unfamiliar
Victories of Samothrace.

The past is not something fixed and unalterable.
Its facts are rediscovered by every succeeding gen-
eration, its values reassessed, its meanings redefined
in the context of present tastes and preoccupations.
Out of the same documents and monuments and
works of art, every epoch invents its own Middle
Ages, its private China, its patented and copy-
righted Hellas. Today, thanks to recent advances in
the technology of lighting, we can go one better
than our predecessors. Not only have we reinter-
preted the great works of sculpture bequeathed to
us by the past, we have actually succeeded in alter-
ing the physical appearance of these works. Greek
statues, as we see them illuminated by a light that
never was on land or sea, and then photographed
in a series of fragmentary close-ups from the oddest
angles, bear almost no resemblance to the Greek
statues seen by art critics and the general public in
the dim galleries and decorous engravings of the
past. The aim of the classical artist, in whatever
period he may happen to live, is to impart order to
the chaos of experience, to present a comprehensible, rational picture of reality, in which all the parts
are clearly seen and coherently related, so that the

beholder knows (or, to be more accurate, imagines that he knows) precisely what's what. To us, this ideal of rational orderliness makes no appeal. Consequently, when we are confronted by works of classical art, we use all the means in our power to make them look like something which they are not, and were never meant to be. From a work, whose whole point is its unity of conception, we select a single feature, focus our searchlights upon it and so force it, out of all context, upon the observer's consciousness. Where a contour seems to us too continuous, too obviously comprehensible, we break it up by alternating impenetrable shadows with patches of glaring brightness. When we photograph a sculptured figure or group, we use the camera to isolate a part, which we then exhibit in enigmatic independence from the whole. By such means we can de-classicize the severest classic. Subjected to the light treatment and photographed by an expert cameraman, a Pheidias becomes a piece of Gothic expressionism, a Praxiteles is turned into a fascinating *surrealist* object dredged up from the ooziest depths of the subconscious. This may be bad art history, but it is certainly enormous fun.

IV

Painter in ordinary, first to the Duke of his native Lorraine and later to the King of France, Georges de Latour was treated, during his lifetime, as the great artist he so manifestly was. With the accession of Louis XIV and the rise, the deliberate cultivation, of a new art of Versailles, aristocratic in subject matter and lucidly classical in style, the reputation of this once famous man suffered an eclipse so complete that, within a couple of generations, his very name had been forgotten, and his surviving paintings came to be attributed to the Lee Nains, to Honthorst, to Zurbarán, to Murillo, even to Velázquez. The rediscovery of Latour began in 1915 and was virtually complete by 1934, when the Louvre organized a notable exhibition of "The Painters of Reality." Ignored for nearly three hundred years, one of the greatest of French painters had come back to claim his rights.

Georges de Latour was one of those extroverted visionaries, whose art faithfully reflects certain aspects of the outer world, but reflects them in a state

of transfiguration, so that every meanest particular
becomes intrinsically significant, a manifestation of
the absolute. Most of his compositions are of figures
seen by the light of a single candle. A single candle,
as Caravaggio and the Spaniards had shown, can
give rise to the most enormous theatrical effects.
But Latour took no interest in theatrical effects.
There is nothing dramatic in his pictures, nothing
tragic or pathetic or grotesque, no representation of
action, no appeal to the sort of emotions, which
people go to the theater to have excited and then
appeased. His personages are essentially static.
They never *do* anything; they are simply *there* in
the same way in which a granite Pharaoh is there,
or a bodhisattva from Khmer, or one of Piero's flat-
footed angels. And the single candle is used, in every
case, to stress this intense but unexcited, impersonal
thereness. By exhibiting common things in an un-
common light, its flame makes manifest the living
mystery and inexplicable marvel of mere existence.
There is so little religiosity in the paintings that in
many cases it is impossible to decide whether we
are confronted by an illustration to the Bible or a
study of models by candlelight. Is the "Nativity" at
Rennes *the* nativity, or merely *a* nativity? Is the
picture of an old man asleep under the eyes of a
young girl merely that? Or is it of St. Peter in prison
being visited by the delivering angel? There is no
way of telling. But though Latour's art is wholly
without religiosity, it remains profoundly religious

in the sense that it reveals, with unexampled intensity, the divine omnipresence.

It must be added that, as a man, this great painter of God's immanence seems to have been proud, hard, intolerably overbearing and avaricious. Which goes to show, yet once more, that there is never a one-to-one correspondence between an artist's work and his character.

V

At the near point Vuillard panited interiors for the most part, but sometimes also gardens. In a few compositions he managed to combine the magic of propinquity with the magic of remoteness by representing a corner of a room in which there stands or hangs one of his own, or someone else's, representations of a distant view of trees, hills and sky. It is an invitation to make the best of both worlds, the telescopic and the microscopic, at a single glance.

For the rest, I can think of only a very few close-up landscapes by modern European artists. There is a strange "Thicket" by Van Gogh at the Metropolitan. There is Constable's wonderful "Dell in Helmington Park" at the Tate. There is a bad picture, Millais's "Ophelia," made magical, in spite of everything, by its intricacies of summer greenery seen from the point of view, very nearly, of a water rat. And I remember a Delacroix, glimpsed long ago at some loan exhibition, of bark and leaves and blossom at the closest range. There must, of course, be others; but either I have forgotten, or have never seen them. In any case there is nothing in the West comparable to the Chinese and Japanese renderings of nature at the near point. A spray of blossoming plum, eighteen inches of a bamboo stem with its leaves, tits or finches seen at hardly more than arm's length among the bushes, all kinds of flowers and foliage, of birds and fish and small mammals. Each tiny life is represented as the center of its own universe, the purpose, in its own estimation, for which this world and all that is in it were created; each issues its own specific and individual declaration of independence from human imperialism; each, by ironic implication, derides our absurd pretensions to lay down merely human rules for the conduct of the cosmic game; each mutely repeats the divine tautology: I am that I am.

Nature at the middle distance is familiar—so familiar that we are deluded into believing that we really know what it is all about. Seen very close at hand, or at a great distance, or from an odd angle, it seems disquietingly strange, wonderful beyond all comprehension. The close-up landscapes of China and Japan are so many illustrations of the theme that samsara and nirvana are one, that the Absolute is manifest in every appearance. These great metaphysical, and yet pragmatic, truths were rendered by the Zen-inspired artists of the Far East in yet another way. All the objects of their near-point scrutiny were represented in a state of unrelatedness against a blank of virgin silk or paper. Thus isolated, these transient appearances take on a kind of absolute Thing-in-Itselfhood. Western artists have used this device when painting sacred figures, portraits and, sometimes, natural objects at a distance. Rembrandt's "Mill" and Van Gogh's "Cypresses" are examples of long-range landscapes in which a single feature has been absolutized by isolation. The magical power of many of Goya's etchings, drawings and paintings can be accounted for by the fact that his compositions almost always take the form of a few silhouettes, or even a single silhouette, seen against a blank. These silhouetted shapes possess the visionary quality of intrinsic significance, heightened by isolation and unrelatedness to preternatural intensity. In nature, as in a work of art, the isolation of an object tends to invest it with absoluteness, to endow it with that more-than-symbolic meaning which is identical with being.

> —But there's a Tree—of many, *one*,
> A *single* Field which I have looked upon,
> Both of them speak of something that is gone.

The something which Wordsworth could no longer see was the "visionary gleam." That gleam, I remember, and that intrinsic significance were the properties of a solitary oak that could be seen from the train, between Reading and Oxford, growing from the summit of a little knoll in a wide expanse of plowland, and silhouetted against the pale northern sky.

The effects of isolation combined with proximity

may be studied, in all their magical strangeness, in an extraordinary painting by a seventeenth-century Japanese artist, who was also a famous swordsman and a student of Zen. It represents a butcherbird, perched on the very tip of a naked branch, "waiting without purpose, but in the state of highest tension." Beneath, above and all around is nothing. The bird emerges from the Void, from that eternal nameless-ness and formlessness, which is yet the very sub-stance of the manifold, concrete and transient uni-verse. That shrike on its bare branch is first cousin to Hardy's wintry thrush. But whereas the thrush insists on teaching us some kind of a lesson, the Far Eastern butcherbird is content simply to exist, to be intensely and absolutely there.

VI

Many schizophrenics pass most of their time neither
on earth, nor in heaven, nor even in hell, but in a
gray, shadowy world of phantoms and unreal-
ities. What is true of these psychotics is true, to a
lesser extent, of certain neurotics afflicted by a
milder form of mental illness. Recently it has been
found possible to induce this state of ghostly existence by administering a small quantity of one of the
derivatives of adrenalin. For the living, the doors of
heaven, hell and limbo are opened, not by "massy
keys of metals twain," but by the presence in the
blood of one set of chemical compounds and the
absence of another set. The shadow world inhabited by some schizophrenics and neurotics closely
resembles the world of the dead, as described in
some of the earlier religious traditions. Like the
wraiths in Sheol and in Homer's Hades, these men-
tally disturbed persons have lost touch with matter,
language and their fellow beings. They have no
purchase on life and are condemned to ineffective-

ness, solitude and a silence broken only by the senseless squeak and gibber of ghosts.

The history of eschatological ideas marks a genuine progress—a progress which can be described
in theological terms as the passage from Hades to
Heaven, in chemical terms as the substitution of
mescalin and lysergic acid for adrenolutin, and in
psychological terms as the advance from catatonia
and feelings of unreality to a sense of heightened
reality in vision and, finally, in mystical experience.

VII

Géricault was a negative visionary; for though his art was almost obsessively true to nature, it was true to a nature that had been magically transfigured, in his perceiving and rendering of it, for the worse. "I start to paint a woman," he once said, "but it always ends up as a lion." More often, indeed, it ended up as something a good deal less amiable than a lion— as a corpse, for example, as a demon. His master-piece, the prodigious "Raft of the *Medusa*," was painted not from life, but from dissolution and decay—from bits of cadavers supplied by medical students, from the emaciated torso and jaundiced face of a friend who was suffering from a disease of the liver. Even the waves on which the raft is floating, even the overarching sky are corpse-colored. It is as though the entire universe had become a dissecting room.

And then there are his demonic pictures. "The Derby," it is obvious, is being run in hell, against a background fairly blazing with darkness visible. "The Horse Startled by Lightning," in the National

Gallery, is the revelation, in a single frozen instant,
of the strangeness, the sinister and even infernal
otherness that hides in familiar things. In the Metropolitan Museum there is a portrait of a child. And
what a child! In his luridly brilliant jacket the little
darling is what Baudelaire liked to call "a budding
Satan," *un Satan en herbe*. And the study of a naked
man, also in the Metropolitan, is none other than
the budding Satan grown up.

From the accounts which his friends have left of
him it is evident that Géricault habitually saw the
world about him as a succession of visionary apocalypses. The prancing horse of his early "Officer de
Chasseurs" was seen one morning, on the road to
Saint Cloud, in a dusty glare of summer sunshine,
rearing and plunging between the shafts of an om-
nibus. The personages in the "Raft of the *Medusa*"
were painted in finished detail, one by one, on the
virgin canvas. There was no outline drawing of the
whole composition, no gradual building up of an
overall harmony of tones and hues. Each particular
revelation—of a body in decay, of a sick man in the
ghastly extremity of hepatitis—was fully rendered
as it was seen and artistically realized. By a miracle
of genius, every successive apocalypse was made to
fit, prophetically, into a harmonious whole, which
existed, when the earlier of the appalling visions
were transferred to canvas, only in the artist's imagination.

VIII

In *Sartor Resartus* Carlyle has left what (in *Mr. Carlyle, My Patient*) his psychosomatic biographer, Dr. James Halliday, calls "an amazing description of a psychotic state of mind, largely depressive, but partly schizophrenic."

"The men and women around me," writes Carlyle, "even speaking too with me, were but Figures; I had practically forgotten that they were alive, that they were not merely automata. Friendship was but an incredible tradition. In the midst of their crowded streets and assemblages I walked solitary; and (except that it was my own heart, not another's, that I kept devouring) savage also as the tiger in the jungle. . . . To me the Universe was all void of Life, of Purpose, of Volition, even of Hostility; it was one huge, dead, immeasurable Steam-Engine, rolling on in its dead indifference, to grind me limb from limb . . . Having no hope, neither had I any definite fear, were it of Man or of Devil. And yet, strangely enough, I lived in a continual, indefinite, pining fear, tremulous, pusillanimous, apprehensive of I knew not what; it seemed as if all things in the Heavens above, and the Earth beneath, would hurt me; as if the Heavens and the Earth were but boundless jaws of a devouring Monster, wherein I, palpitating, waited to be devoured." Renée and the idolater of heroes are evidently describing the same experience. Infinity is apprehended by both, but in the form of "the System," the "immeasurable Steam-Engine." To both, again, all is significant, but negatively significant, so that every event is utterly pointless, every object intensely unreal, every self-styled human being a clockwork dummy, grotesquely going through the motions of work and play, of loving, hating, thinking, of being eloquent, heroic, saintly, what you will—the robots are nothing if not versatile.